I wrote this book during the 2020 COVID-19 lockdown, a time
of fear, loss, and social unrest, when my then two-year-old son
couldn't leave our apartment for months. I dedicate this book to
all of those kids who had to spend an eternity indoors. I hope it
helps to remind us all of the need for access to wild spaces.
ICO ROMERO REYES

To my sister Astrid, who has always shone a light on my path.
TÀNIA GARCÍA

Translated from the Spanish *Veneno*

First published in the United Kingdom in 2022 by
Thames & Hudson Ltd, 181A High Holborn, London WC1V 7QX

First published in the United States of America in 2022 by
Thames & Hudson Inc., 500 Fifth Avenue, New York, New York 10110

Original edition © 2021 Mosquito Books, Barcelona
Text © 2021 Ico Romero
Illustrations © 2021 Tània García
This edition © 2022 Thames & Hudson Ltd, London

British Library Cataloguing-in-Publication Data.
A catalogue record for this book is available from the British Library

Library of Congress Control Number 2021952602

ISBN 978-0-500-65291-6

Printed in Spain

ICO ROMERO • TÀNIA GARCÍA

TOXIC

The World's Deadliest Creatures

CONTENTS

2

Before you dive into this spine-tingling collection of creatures, become a poison expert! Here are some of the basic ideas you'll find in this book.

WHAT IS POISON?

A poison is a substance that can cause harm, illness, or death to living things. Poisons can be found all around in nature—in minerals, plants, or animals. Many species from all across the animal kingdom use poison to protect themselves from predators, or to capture prey.

HOW DO POISONS WORK?

Poisons affect the way that your body works. For example, some affect the nervous system, stopping the nerves from sending signals to your heart or brain. They may stop your heart or prevent you from breathing properly. Others affect the body's circulation system. Blood won't clot properly and wounds will keep bleeding.

THE DOSE MAKES THE POISON

A poison needs to be given in a large enough amount before it will harm its victim. Even harmless substances like water or salt can be deadly if consumed in huge quantities. Some poisons are very powerful—just a tiny drop can kill. Others may need to collect in the body before they can do any damage.

The amount of poison needed to have an effect also depends on the size of the victim. That is why poison is especially dangerous to children, who are smaller.

THE TARGET MAKES THE POISON, TOO

Poisons produced by animals are usually intended to hurt their predators or prey, leaving other species unharmed. Some animals can eat other poisonous creatures—instead of getting sick, their bodies store the poison and can reuse it, so they become poisonous themselves.

WHAT IS A TOXIN?

Toxins are poisons produced by a living organism, which could be a plant or an animal. Toxins produced by animals are called zootoxins and they come in two forms—poison or venom.

POISON OR VENOM—WHAT'S THE DIFFERENCE?

Is a creature poisonous or venomous? Poison and venom can have similar effects, but they are not the same thing. It all depends on how the animal delivers its toxins.

Poisonous

Poisonous animals have toxins inside parts of their body, like their skin or muscles. When these toxins are eaten, absorbed or inhaled, they cause damage. A trick to remember which animals are poisonous is that **they will harm you if you bite them!**

Venomous

Venomous animals produce toxins and inject them into their victims by stinging or biting. These animals usually have a gland that makes the poison, and a sharp organ to inject it. A trick to remember which animals are venomous is that **they will harm you if they bite (or sting) you!**

TAKE YOUR POISON WITH A PINCH OF SALT

All statements about the power of poison must be considered with care, including the ones in this book! Because poisoning humans would not be legal, scientists use lab mice—or human cells in a glass dish—to test how dangerous a poison is. But poison has different effects on different species and on different organs.

This means it's hard to know how it will affect the human body. Even when a poison or venom is known to be deadly to humans, think— are the animals that produce it common or rare? Do they live where people live? Are they likely to bite? Is there an antidote?

Now that you are a poison expert, let's meet some animals.

ORGANIZING ALL LIVING THINGS

Taxonomy is a system that scientists use to help them understand how all living things are related to each other. Similar forms of life are grouped together into a set of categories that get more specific each time. The largest category, kingdom, contains all animals but not plants or fungi, which have their own kingdoms. The smallest category, species, contains just one type of animal.

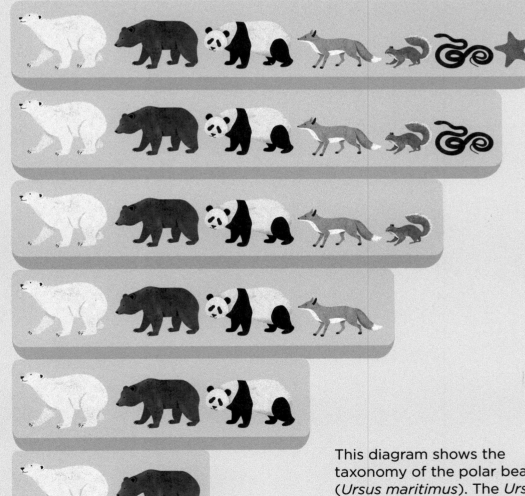

KINGDOM: ANIMALIA

PHYLUM: CHORDATA

CLASS: MAMMALIA

ORDER: CARNIVORA

FAMILY: URSIDAE

GENUS: URSUS

SPECIES: MARITIMUS

Ursus maritimus

Polar bear

This diagram shows the taxonomy of the polar bear (*Ursus maritimus*). The *Ursidae* family includes (among others) polar bears, brown bears and pandas. The genus *Ursus* includes brown bears and polar bears but not pandas. The species *Ursus maritimus* includes only polar bears.

POISON DART FROGS

Small, deadly and brightly colored, these frogs from the *Dentrobatidae* family are among the most poisonous animals in the world. They live in the tropical rainforests of Central and South America.

THE REASON FOR THE NAME

The Embera-Wounaan people of Colombia traditionally used the toxin from these frogs to poison the tips of blow-gun darts, which they used for hunting.

TINY BUT BRIGHT

Poison dart frogs can be as small as half an inch but this doesn't mean they're hard to spot. Their bold colors and patterns are a way of warning away predators.

WHY SO DANGEROUS?

The bodies of these frogs contain batrachotoxin, a very poisonous substance. It is not made by the frogs themselves and may come from the rainforest insects that they eat. The *Dentrobatidae* family also includes frog species that are less colorful and less toxic.

FROGS IN DANGER

Golden dart frogs have only one predator—the fire-bellied snake. It is immune to their poison and can eat them safely. Nowadays, habitat loss and smugglers are these frogs' biggest enemies.

GOLD MEDAL

The most dangerous member of the family is the golden dart frog (*Phyllobates terribilis*). It's probably the most toxic species on Earth. One frog could kill 10 to 20 adult humans.

VENOMOUS MAMMALS

Venomous mammals are rare, but they prove you should never jump to conclusions about a creature, even if it looks cute and furry!

SLOW LORIS

This big-eyed animal is the only venomous primate in the world, and it is endangered. If you've ever dreamed of petting cute animals in the wild, the slow loris shows why this is not a good idea! When a loris feels threatened, it raises its arms above its head and quickly licks its armpits. The glands under its arms produce a venomous sweat-like liquid, and when this liquid mixes with the loris's spit, it becomes even more powerful. The loris usually delivers the venom by biting, but it can also rub it on its fur. It's not deadly to humans but can cause a nasty swelling.

COMMON VAMPIRE BAT

This bat got its name because it drinks the blood of mammals, including cows and sheep. It comes out at night, crawling on all fours to approach its prey. Then it clings onto them and bites through their skin with its razor-sharp teeth. The vampire bat's saliva contains a mild venom, which stops the blood from clotting while it's feeding.

PLATYPUS

This unusual creature is one of only two mammals that lay eggs. As if that wasn't strange enough, male platypuses have venomous spurs on their back feet. The spurs are used only during the platypus breeding season, when the males fight over the females. The venom is strong enough to kill a dog and is very painful to humans.

9

CORAL AND SEA ANEMONES

A GANG OF STINGERS

Cnidaria is a phylum of sea animals that includes corals, sea anemones and jellyfish. Their bodies all contain special stinging cells, which are called cnidocytes.

THE LEGEND OF THE DEADLY POOL

According to a Hawaiian legend, a shark god ate several people from a village on the island of Maui. In revenge, the villagers killed the god and spread his ashes in a tide pool. Soon after, a plant began to grow there. The local people called it "Limu-make-o-Hana," which means "deadly seaweed of Hana." It was so toxic that it was used to poison the tips of spears.

The site became a sacred place, and its location was kept secret for a long time. Scientists began to study this pool in the 1960s. In it, they found a type of coral that they named *Palythoa toxica* (below). This coral produces one of the most toxic substances on Earth, palytoxin.

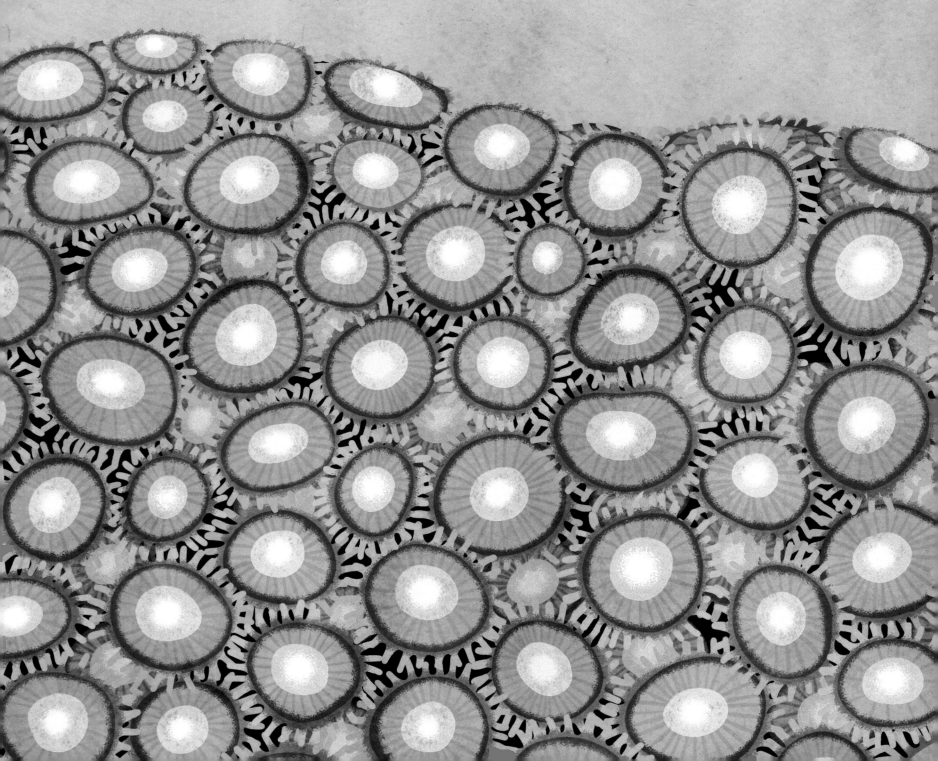

THE TOXIC BEAUTY OF SEA ANEMONES

Although they are named after a flower, sea anemones are animals, not plants. They attach themselves to rocks and catch prey with their waving tentacles. Each tentacle is covered with tiny stinging harpoon-like spikes, loaded with paralyzing venom. However, one creature is immune to this attack—the clownfish. Its skin is covered by a sticky layer of mucus that protects it from the sea anemone's sting. This means it can hide among the anemone's tentacles and stay safe from other predators. There are more than a thousand species of sea anemones, but only ten of them have this kind of special relationship, each with a particular type of clownfish.

TOXIC BIRDS

POISONOUS PLUMAGE

No venomous birds have ever been discovered, but there are a very small number of birds that are poisonous. Poisonous birds absorb toxins from the world around them, probably through their food. Some scientists think that these toxins are used as a form of protection from predators. Others believe that they help to keep away parasites. It's possible that both of these ideas are correct.

HOODED PITOHUI

While handling birds in New Guinea in the 1990s, one scientist was scratched by a bird called a hooded pitohui. The scratch hurt, and when he put the cut to his mouth, his mouth started tingling and went numb. When the research team asked the local people about these birds, they explained that the "garbage birds" (as they call them) taste very bad and are also poisonous. The scientists did some experiments and learned that hooded pitohuis contain small amounts of batrachotoxin, the same toxin that is found in poison dart frogs. This made the hooded pitohui the first poisonous bird ever discovered.

BLUE-CAPPED IFRIT

The bird-hunters of New Guinea also avoid the blue-capped ifrit. The Kairon and Simbai people call it the "bitter bird." When the ifrit is eaten, its meat creates a burning sensation that feels like an extremely strong chilli pepper.

ARE BEETLES TO BLAME?

The forests of New Guinea are also home to beetles from the genus *Choresine*. Their bodies contain high levels of toxins and have been found in the birds' stomachs. There is a good chance that eating these beetles is what makes these birds poisonous.

GILA MONSTER

A RARE CLUB

Gila monsters are lizards that live in the deserts of Mexico and the southwestern United States. They are one of the two surviving descendants of *Monsterosauria*, an ancient group of predatory lizards that lived in tropical climates. These cold-blooded creatures have thick skins covered in beadlike bumps. This type of skin was common among dinosaurs but is rare among modern reptiles.

TOO DRY FOR COMFORT

Gila monsters have been called a "crawling contradiction." They live in the desert but their ancestors came from tropical places so their skin needs moisture. This means that they don't seem well suited to desert life, but somehow they manage to survive there.

A VENOMOUS BITE

The Gila monster has powerful jaws and razor-sharp teeth. Its venom flows down grooves in the sides of its teeth. Its chewing bite is very painful but rarely fatal to humans.

LAYING LOW

These reptiles spend up to 90% of their time underground. They come out during the day in springtime, and at night in the rainy season. In the spring, they gather together to find a mate.

FAST OR FEAST

Gila monsters can survive for a whole year on just three big meals—usually eggs or baby mammals. Young Gila monsters can eat 50% of their own body weight in one go. They store fat in their thick tails and can use their bladders to store enough water to survive for 90 days.

GREATER BLUE-RINGED OCTOPUS

A QUIET LIFE?

The greater blue-ringed octopus lives in the shallow waters of the Indian and Pacific Oceans. It's fairly small—around the size of a golf ball—and usually pretty shy. It stays close to the rocky crevices where it lives, only coming out to feed or mate. Its skin is covered in color-changing cells called chromatophores, which it uses to camouflage itself. Most of the time, it prefers to go unnoticed.

BLUE ALERT

When the blue-ringed octopus is threatened, however, it goes through a transformation. It stops imitating the brown rocks around it and switches on its glowing blue rings, flashing them on and off like an amazing light show. The blue rings are a message to predators that means "I'm toxic—stay away!"

A DEADLY DISPLAY

The greater blue-ringed octopus is one of the most venomous sea creatures. Its deadly venom comes from bacteria that live in the octopus's saliva glands. A bite from the horny beak of the octopus is painless, but can kill a human in minutes.

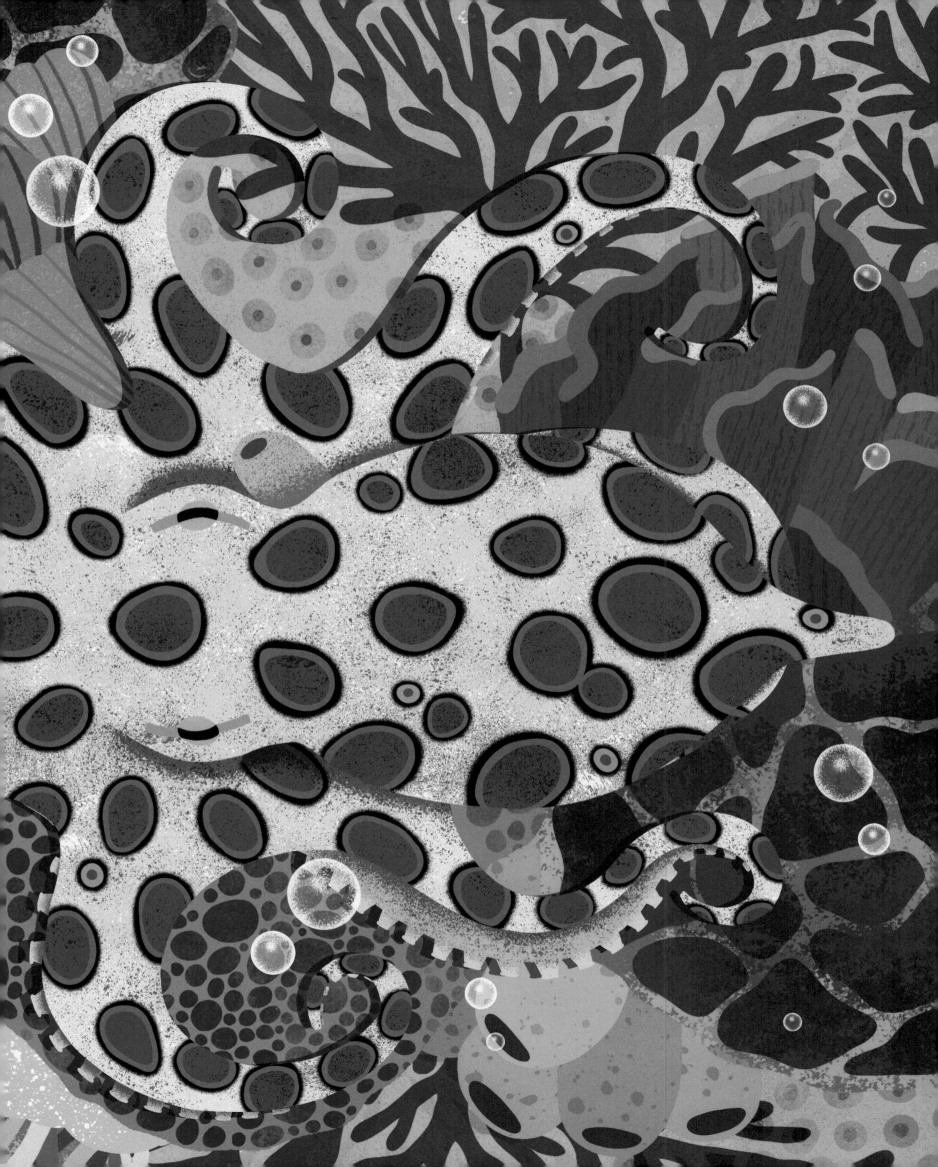

SNAKES

Snakes are often the first animal that comes to mind when people think about venom. Throughout history, snakes have been important symbols in many cultures. In Greek mythology, the god of healing and medicine Asclepius carried a rod with a snake curled around it. In the Christian tradition, snakes are linked with the ideas of darkness and temptation. In Buddhism, they are a symbol of protection, and in Hinduism, they represent life, death and rebirth.

ALL ABOUT SNAKES

Snakes are scaly reptiles with no legs. They come in many different sizes and live in a wide range of environments, including land, sea and freshwater. Young snakes shed their skin about four times a year. Most snake species are not venomous, but some have venom powerful enough to hurt or kill humans.

INLAND TAIPAN

Also known as the fierce snake, the inland taipan has the most toxic venom of any snake. It specializes in hunting mammals and its bite is fatal to humans. Fortunately, it lives only in the remote deserts of central Australia and is very rare. It was spotted by a scientist in 1882, then it wasn't seen again until 1972, ninety years later!

BLACK MAMBA

The black mamba is fast and good at climbing. Its venomous bite can easily kill a human. It lives in the bushlands of central Africa and can reach a length of 13 feet, and a speed of 9 miles an hour. Black mamba venom is very powerful and causes many deaths in places where the antidote is not available.

KING COBRA

Imagine a snake charmer playing a pipe and a hooded snake rising out of a basket. You are probably picturing one of the most famous snakes on earth—the king cobra. King cobras are the longest of all venomous snakes. They can also raise one third of their body length off the ground, making them tall enough to look a human adult in the eye. Their venom is powerful enough to kill an adult elephant with a single bite.

BELCHER'S SEA SNAKE

Belcher's sea snake is very venomous but also fairly shy. It lives on coral reefs and feeds by ambushing other sea creatures. Although it lives in the ocean, it can't breathe underwater. However, it can spend up to eight hours below the surface before coming up for air.

This snake is hunted in Thailand and Vietnam, where it is a popular ingredient in soups, drinks and traditional medicines. Most people bitten by it are fishermen or snake handlers.

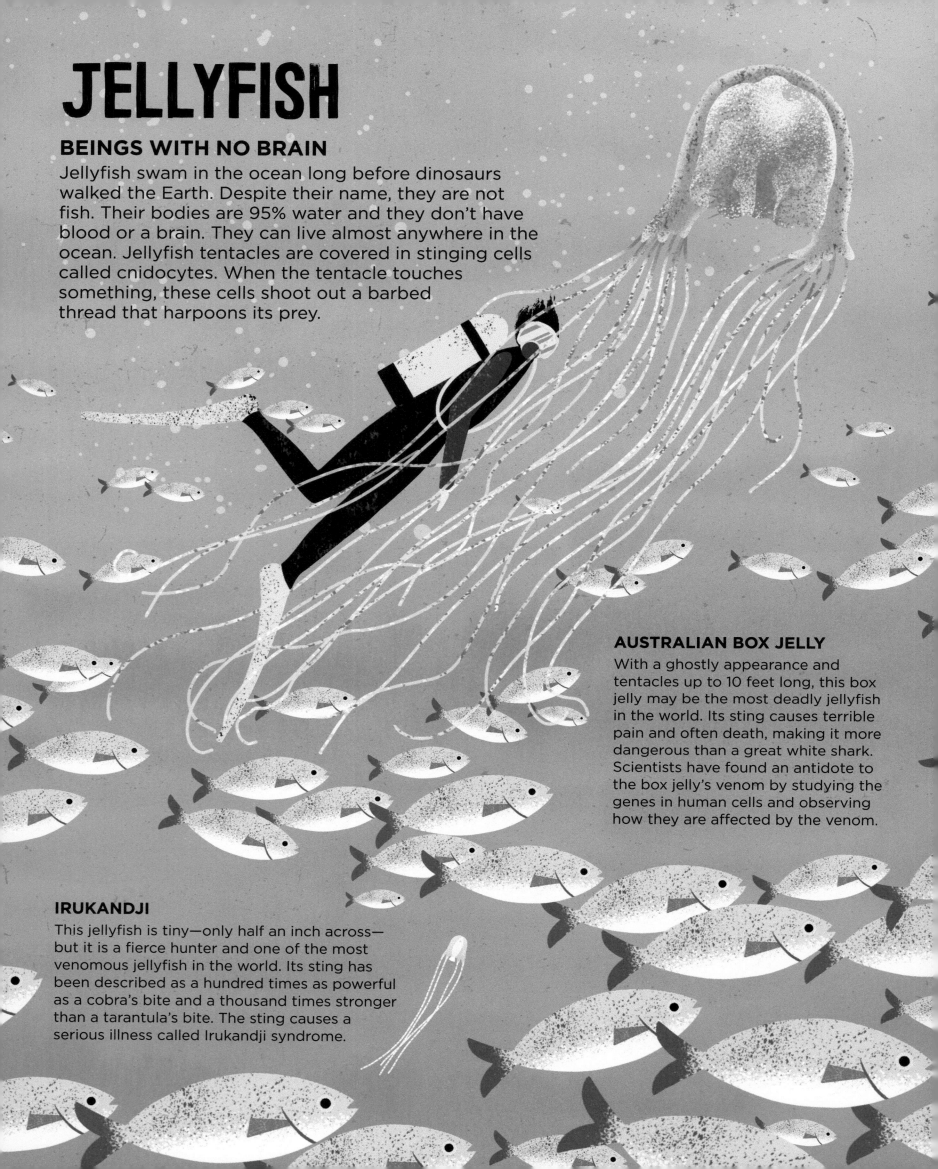

JELLYFISH

BEINGS WITH NO BRAIN

Jellyfish swam in the ocean long before dinosaurs walked the Earth. Despite their name, they are not fish. Their bodies are 95% water and they don't have blood or a brain. They can live almost anywhere in the ocean. Jellyfish tentacles are covered in stinging cells called cnidocytes. When the tentacle touches something, these cells shoot out a barbed thread that harpoons its prey.

AUSTRALIAN BOX JELLY

With a ghostly appearance and tentacles up to 10 feet long, this box jelly may be the most deadly jellyfish in the world. Its sting causes terrible pain and often death, making it more dangerous than a great white shark. Scientists have found an antidote to the box jelly's venom by studying the genes in human cells and observing how they are affected by the venom.

IRUKANDJI

This jellyfish is tiny—only half an inch across—but it is a fierce hunter and one of the most venomous jellyfish in the world. Its sting has been described as a hundred times as powerful as a cobra's bite and a thousand times stronger than a tarantula's bite. The sting causes a serious illness called Irukandji syndrome.

PACIFIC SEA NETTLE

This Pacific Ocean jellyfish spreads its tentacles like a net and drifts along, waiting for its next meal. The frilly white tentacles in its center are called "oral arms" and are used to carry prey to its mouth. Its sting is painful but not deadly to humans.

TOXIC FISH

In the forms of both venom and poison, toxins are common under the sea. Fish are no exception.

STONEFISH

Camouflaged on the sea bed, the stonefish waits quietly until its prey swims by, then attacks at lightning speed. Stonefish live in the Indian and Pacific Oceans and are the most venomous fish on Earth. They have thirteen spines down their back. Each spine works like a syringe, with a sharp tip and two venom sacs that squirt out toxins. The spines are so strong that they can pierce a boot.

LIONFISH

Lionfish is the common name of *Pterois*, a genus of venomous sea fish. Lionfish have beautiful stripes and their back and fins are covered in long venomous spikes. They are native to the Indian and Pacific Oceans but are now invading other sea areas because they have so few predators. Although they are venomous, humans can eat lionfish if they are prepared and cooked correctly—they are surprisingly tasty!

PUFFERFISH

The *Tetraodontidae* family includes more than 120 species of pufferfish. They live in tropical waters and are very toxic. They are the third most poisonous vertebrate animal, after poison dart frogs and stonefish. Pufferfish get their name from their ability to puff up their bodies into a round balloon shape, so predators can't bite them. Although they are poisonous, some species are eaten in Japan. It's tricky to remove the poison, however, so only the most skilled chefs can cook this dangerous meal.

ANTS

CIVILIZED SOLDIERS

Ants are unusual creatures. These insects live in social groups, with each ant having a different job to do. They look after each other and they are able to solve complex problems by working together. Over 70% of the known species of ants can sting, bite, or spray venom. Ants use their venom to hunt prey, compete with other ants, and protect their nests from predators or diseases. Some species of ants are even able to kill an elephant by stinging it again and again.

BULLET ANT

This ant is the most painful insect to be stung by. Their sting is said to feel like being shot with a bullet. If it feels threatened, a single bullet ant will attack. At the same time, it releases a chemical signal that tells other ants to start stinging.

GIANT RED BULL ANT

The giant red bull ant can be more than an inch long. It has jagged mandibles (mouth parts) and a venomous sting. Unlike most ants, red bull ants don't use chemicals to sense the world. However, they are one of the few ant species with very good eyesight.

LEMON ANT

Lemon ants make a poison that kills most plants that grow in the Amazon rainforest. This creates clear patches in the forest, known as "devil's gardens." The only plants that survive in these clearings are called myrmecophytes, which means "ant plants."

These plants grow special hollow "pods" on their stems where the ants can live, breed, and grow fungus to eat. The plants and the ants survive by protecting each other. This kind of shared relationship is called symbiosis.

SPIDERS

Spinning webs and scuttling in the dark, spiders are often thought to be dangerous and scary, but this reputation is very unfair. Scientists have recorded 45,000 spider species, but there may be as many as 170,000 species in the world. All of them produce venom, but very few spiders are dangerous to humans. It's true that most spiders are predators, but they eat an estimated 450 to 900 million tons of insects each year. That's an amazing pest control service!

SYDNEY FUNNEL-WEB SPIDER

It's big, glossy, and dark, and has a powerful pair of fangs. *Atrax robustus* is the holder of the world record for the most venomous spider. Its venom is extremely toxic to humans and monkeys but relatively harmless to other mammals. Funnel-web spiders get their name from the shape of their home, a funnel-shaped burrow with a web of trip-lines around its entrance. The spider waits near the entrance until a potential victim trips one of the lines, then it pounces.

THE INSECT SMOOTHIE DIET

Almost all spiders are carnivores. Instead of eating their prey straight away, they spit or inject stomach juices into it. These juices turn the insides of the prey to liquid. The spiders then suck it up, like drinking juice from a box!

SILK SKILLS

All spiders make silk and they use it in lots of different ways. As well as spinning webs, they use it to build burrows or nests in the ground, as a cocoon to protect their eggs, as a rope to tie up their prey, as a bungee cord, or even as a parachute!

SPIDER SENSES

Spiders don't have ears or noses like we do. Instead, they use the hairs on their legs to hear, feel, and smell.

BRAZILIAN WANDERING SPIDERS

These large spiders found in Central and South America belong to a genus called *Phoneutria*, which means "murderess" in Greek. They are called wandering spiders because they don't live in webs or burrows. Instead, they wander the forest, hunting for food. When threatened, they lift up their front four legs to show off their colors and make themselves look bigger. Their venom may have important medical uses and has been studied for over sixty years.

TARANTULA VERSUS WASP

On one side of the arena, the huge and hairy tarantula, a spider that can eat birds and mice! On the opposite side, the spider wasp, with its long thin stinger that gives the one of the most painful stings in the world! Who will win the battle? The pair wrestle for control, pushing and pulling each other. Suddenly, the wasp grabs the tarantula, flips it onto its back and stings. The tarantula is paralyzed by the venom! The wasp takes the helpless tarantula to a burrow and lays its eggs on the spider's body. When the wasp larvae hatch, they feed on the spider. Despite its fierce reputation, the tarantula never stood much of a chance.

SCORPIONS

Scorpions are not insects. Like spiders, they belong to a group of animals called arachnids. They have been around for 435 million years and have adapted to live in some of the toughest environments on Earth. Some scorpions live in deserts where the temperature switches from freezing cold to scorching hot. If they need to, they can survive without food for a year.

EMPEROR SCORPION

This large scorpion with huge claws is native to West Africa. It's not fierce and mostly uses its pincers for self-defense—only young emperor scorpions use their stingers. This scorpion mainly eats insects, especially termites, with the occasional treat of a mouse or lizard.

BAD REPUTATION

Although people are often scared of scorpions, they are rarely deadly. There are almost 2,000 scorpion species, but only between 25 and 40 have venom that can harm humans. Most are only a threat to the insects and other small creatures that they feed on.

UNIQUE PHYSIQUE

Scorpions can be easily recognized by their two pincer claws at the front and their curved tail at the back, which has a venomous stinger. As a general rule, the scorpions with the most powerful stingers tend to have smaller claws, and vice versa.

INDIAN RED SCORPION

The sting of the Indian red scorpion can be fatal to humans. It is particularly dangerous to children who live in the same area and might accidentally disturb it. Luckily, a lifesaving anti-venom has been discovered.

CONE SNAILS

DEADLY SEASHELLS BY THE SEASHORE

A sea snail that hides inside a beautifully patterned shell, the cone snail lives in tropical and subtropical waters near coral reefs. Although it may look innocent, it has a powerful venom and a harpoon-like tooth that it uses to sting its prey—or any careless beach visitor who might get too close!

SNEAKY SNAIL

Cone snails are predators, but their bodies are slow and clumsy. A fast and deadly attack is their key to survival. When they detect the scent of prey, they stretch out a long hollow tube with a sharp harpoon on the end. Venom travels down the tube and fills the harpoon. Sea creatures hit by the harpoon are immediately paralyzed. If they are small enough, the cone snail swallows them whole.

A TOXIC COCKTAIL

The venom of cone snails is unique. Each cone snail species produces about 500 toxic chemicals that are mixed together to make its venom. There are around 500 known species of cone snails. That makes roughly 250,000 unique "recipes" for venom that interact with the body in different ways. Scientists are studying them because some could be very useful in medical treatments.

AN EXTRA DOSE OF POISON

BECOME A TOXINOLOGIST

Toxinologists are scientists who study toxins and the living things that produce them. If you are fascinated by poisonous and venomous animals, this may be the right job for you!

WHAT KIND OF THINGS DOES A TOXINOLOGIST DO?

You might find yourself hunting for poison dart frogs in the rainforest or diving for cone snails. On another day, you could milk a stonefish for its venom, or make a slow-motion video to observe how a jellyfish stings. You could also study the different chemicals that make up a toxin. If you're very lucky, you may even invent a new medical use for venom or create an anti-venom. It is quite a job!

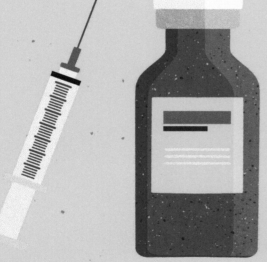
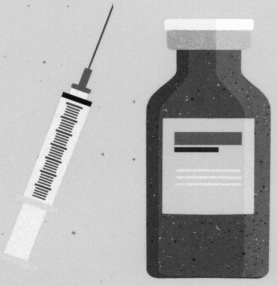

CAN POISONOUS ANIMALS POISON THEMSELVES?

There are two main ways that animals avoid being affected by their own poison. Firstly, they store the poison in a safe and well-insulated place inside their body. Alternatively, they can develop a resistance to it.

STOPPING THE EFFECTS OF VENOM

What is an anti-venom?

Anti-venom is a type of medicine used to treat the effects of venom in the body.

How are anti-venoms made?

Anti-venoms are made in a similar way to vaccines. First, a low dose of venom is given to a domestic animal. Horses are most commonly used for this because they are big, strong, and safe to work with. In response to the venom, the animal's body creates natural defenses called antibodies. These antibodies are collected, concentrated, and preserved. This anti-venom can then be injected as an antidote to the venom.

What can go wrong?

Anti-venoms take a long time and are expensive to make. The human body sometimes rejects some of the animal components in them, creating an allergic reaction.

A one-man library

For over 30 years, one American man has been injecting himself with venom from snakes, developing immunity to it. This very dangerous habit attracted the attention of scientists, who had never before found so many venom antibodies in one human. The scientists created a library of the man's antibodies and studied his DNA. Using this information, they hope to come up with a new way to make antibodies in a lab, without the use of animals.

HEALTHY, SICK, OR DEAD?

Here is a game to test your poison knowledge. In the situations described below, can you guess how the poison will affect the victim? Will they be healthy, sick, or dead? (Of course, in real life, never go near toxic substances, and always respect wildlife!)

A group of dolphins finds a pufferfish. One of them grabs it with its mouth, shakes it, and then passes it on to the next dolphin. Healthy, sick, or dead? Answer: HEALTHY. Young dolphins have been seen playing this unusual game, and they don't get sick from it. Some scientists even think that the dolphins may even feel drunk from the low doses of toxin.

Someone accidentally eats snake venom. Healthy, sick, or dead? Answer: HEALTHY. Most snakes are venomous, not poisonous. Although the venom would hurt you if it was injected by a bite or a sting, it's harmless if eaten.

A fish swims by a rock and gets stung by a cone snail. Healthy, sick, or dead? Answer: DEAD. The fish is immediately paralyzed by the cone snail's venom. Then the snail crawls out of its shell and swallows the fish whole.

A grasshopper mouse eats a bark scorpion. Healthy, sick, or dead? Answer: HEALTHY. This little rodent eats scorpions that have a very nasty sting. How does it do it? The mouse has evolved so that its body blocks the pain of the scorpion's sting, so it feels fine.

Someone accidentally eats blue-ringed octopus venom. Healthy, sick, or dead? Answer: DEAD. Although eating venom doesn't usually hurt you, there's an exception to every rule. The toxin in the octopus's venom is also a poison—it's the same toxin that can kill you if you eat a pufferfish. So someone who eats blue-ringed octopus venom won't live to tell the tale.

A harlequin poison dart frog jumps out of its tank. Without thinking, the owner catches it with his bare hands. Healthy, sick, or dead? Answer: It depends. If the frog was bought recently, there is a chance that it was poached from the wild and its body may still contain some toxins. If the frog was bought from a responsible breeder, the owner is safe because the frog has never been fed a toxic diet. Poaching is a threat to endangered species and is also dangerous for humans.

GLOSSARY

Anti-venom: A type of medicine that is used to treat the effects of venom.

Arachnids: A group of invertebrate animals that includes spiders and scorpions.

Carnivore: An animal that eats other animals.

Chromatophores: Cells in the skin of cold-blooded animals that contain colored and light-reflecting pigments. Octopuses and squid can adjust the size of these cells and so change the color of their skin.

Cnidocytes: Stinging cells that are found on the tentacles of jellyfish, sea anemones, and coral.

DNA: The molecules inside living cells that contain the code for what the cells should do.

Domestic animal: An animal that has been bred and tamed by humans.

Gland: A group of cells in the body that make other substances. For instance, sweat glands make sweat. Some animals have glands that make venom.

Herbivore: An animal that eats plants.

Immune: Protected from the effects of a particular disease or poison.

Invertebrate: An animal without a backbone.

Irukandji syndrome: A very painful condition caused by the sting of some types of jellyfish.

Larva: The young form of an insect. The plural is larvae.

Oral arms: Special tentacles that some types of jellyfish have. They are used to carry food to the jellyfish's mouth.

Paralyze: To stop a person or animal from moving their body or part of it. Some toxins have this effect.

Parasite: An animal or plant that lives on and feeds off another living animal or plant.

Poaching: Illegally capturing, selling, or killing wildlife

Predator: An animal that hunts other animals to eat.

Prey: An animal that is hunted and eaten by other animals.

Saliva: Another word for spit, the watery substance that forms in the mouths of people and animals.

Smuggler: Someone who illegally trades in goods or animals.

Symbiosis: A relationship that has evolved between two different animals or plants, in which they both benefit from living together.

Taxonomy: A system that scientists use to help them understand how all living things are related to each other. See page 5 for a diagram showing the main taxonomic groups.

Toxin: A poison produced by any living organism—plant, animal, or fungus.

Toxinologist: A scientist who studies toxins and the living things that produce them.

Venom: A toxin made by an animal that is injected into its victim by biting or stinging.

Vertebrate: An animal with a backbone.

Zootoxin: A toxin produced by an animal.

ABOUT THE AUTHORS

Ico Romero grew up in the Canary Islands and studied media, design and technology. She has created digital educational media for museums, including the Center of Contemporary Culture of Barcelona and the American Museum of Natural History. She has also worked extensively in climate change education and her work consistently takes into account gender equality and social justice issues. This is her first book.

Tània García is an illustrator and designer from Barcelona. She studied art and design at Escola Massana, Barcelona University. After working for a few years in interior design, she realized that what she was most passionate about was drawing, so she became a self-taught illustrator. Her work includes illustrated children's books, and commercial and product illustrations. She was nominated as a finalist in the World Illustration Awards 2021.